Unit 1

T0302843

Present progressive: *they are* + verb-*ing*

Question				**Answer**				
	Are	the goats	**running**?	Yes,	they	**are**.		*aren't* = *are not*
				No,	they	**aren't**.		
What	**are**	they	**doing**?		They**'re**		**eating**.	*They're* = *They are*

do → doing eat → eating run → running

1 Write.

1. sleep They're sleeping.
2. clean ______.
3. walk ______.
4. jump ______.
5. swim ______.
6. eat ______.

2 Read and write.

1. What ______ the cats doing?
2. ______ they running? Yes, they ______.
3. What are the sheep ______?
4. Are ______ jumping? No, they ______.
5. They ______ sleeping.

3 **Look and write.** Use the picture in Activity 2.

1. Are the cows sleeping? ______________________.
2. What are the cats doing? ______________________.
3. Are the goats jumping? ______________________.
4. What are the horses doing? ______________________.
5. Are the goats eating? ______________________.

4 **Look.** Write questions.

1. ______________________? They're eating.
2. ______________________? Yes, they are. They're eating.
3. ______________________? They're walking.
4. ______________________? They're sleeping.
5. ______________________? Yes, they are. They're jumping.

5 **Look and write.** Open your Student's Book to pp. 148–149. Write 3 questions and answers about the picture.

What are the cats doing? They're sleeping.

____

____

____

want **+ infinitive**

Question					Answer	
Do	you	**want**	**to see**	the cows?	Yes, I do.	*don't = do not*
					No, I don't. I **want to see** the ducks.	
Does	Ivan				Yes, he does.	*doesn't = does not*
					No, he doesn't. He **wants to ride** the horse.	

want + to + action word: *I **want to feed** the goats. He **wants to see** the chicken.*

1 Read. Circle the answer.

1. Do you **want** / **want to** ride a horse?
2. **Do** / **Does** she want to swim?
3. **Do** / **Does** you want to climb a tree?
4. What **do** / **does** your brother want to do?
5. What **do** / **does** you want to do?
6. What does your father **want** / **wanting** to do?

2 Read and write.

1. I __________ to see the cat.
2. __________ you want to see the cow?
3. What __________ Mei want to do?
4. What does Jian __________ to do?
5. He __________ to see the duck.
6. __________ she want to see the goat? No, she __________.
7. What __________ you __________ to do? I want to see the dog.
8. Do you __________ to see the sheep? No, I __________.

3 **Read.** Write questions.

1. ______________________________?
I want to fly in the sky.

2. ______________________________?
She wants to ride a bike.

3. ______________________________?
She wants to crawl on the grass.

4. ______________________________?
No, he doesn't. My father wants to read.

5. ______________________________?
No, I don't. I don't like cats.

4 **Write.** Write questions.

~~in your kitchen~~	in your living room	
at school	with your friends	with your parents

1. What do you want to do in your kitchen?
2. ______________________________?
3. ______________________________?
4. ______________________________?
5. ______________________________?

5 **Read and write.** Answer the questions in Activity 4.

1. I want to cook.
2. ______________________________.
3. ______________________________.
4. ______________________________.
5. ______________________________.

Unit 2

Present progressive, first person plural

<table>
<tr><th colspan="4">Question</th><th colspan="3">Answer</th><th></th></tr>
<tr><td rowspan="3">What</td><td rowspan="3">are</td><td rowspan="3">you</td><td rowspan="3">doing?</td><td rowspan="3">We're</td><td>reading.</td><td></td><td rowspan="3">we're = we are</td></tr>
<tr><td>cutting</td><td>yellow paper.</td></tr>
<tr><td>erasing</td><td>the board.</td></tr>
</table>

Use *we're* verb + *-ing* for actions happening now.

Note that *you* can be used for one person or many people.

1 Look and write.

1. 

What ___are___ you doing?

We're ___cutting___.

2. 

What are you ________________?

We're ________________.

3. 

________________ are you doing?

We're ________________.

2 **Look.** Write sentences.

1. 

2. 

3. 

________________ ________________ ________________

3 **Look and write.** Write questions and answers.

1. 

What are you doing ____________________?

____________________.

2. 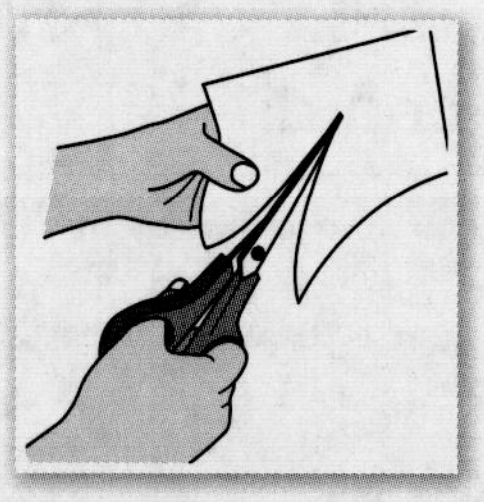

____________________?

____________________.

3. 

____________________?

____________________.

4 **Draw and write.** Draw a picture of your class. Write a question and 2 answers.

____________________?

____________________.

____________________.

Questions with *Are there . . . ?* and short answers

Question				Answer			
Are	**there**	any	crayons?	Yes,	**there**	**are.**	*aren't = are not*
			books?	No,		**aren't.**	

Use *Are there . . . ?* questions to ask about more than one thing.

1 **Read and match.** Draw a line.

1. Are there any
2. How
3. Are
4. No,
5. Yes,
6. Are there

a. there are.
b. notebooks?
c. there aren't.
d. there any paintbrushes?
e. any markers?
f. many erasers?

2 **Read and write.** Think about your classroom.

1. ______________ any pencils on your desk?

______________.

2. ______________ any notebooks in the classroom?

______________.

3. ______________ any erasers on the board?

______________.

4. ______________ any desks in the classroom?

______________.

5. ______________ any balls in the classroom?

______________.

3 **Look.** Write questions.

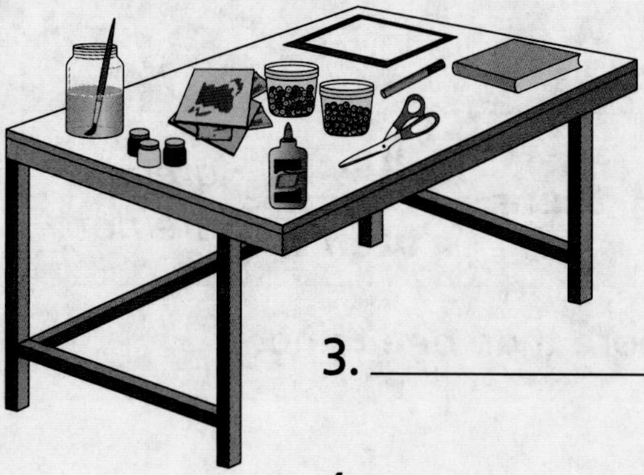

1. Are there any scissors?
2. ______________________
3. ______________________
4. ______________________

4 **Write.** Answer the questions in Activity 3.

1. ______________________ 3. ______________________

2. ______________________ 4. ______________________

5 **Look and write.** Ask questions. Then answer them.

1. Are there any paintbrushes? Yes, there are.
2. ______________________ ______________________
3. ______________________ ______________________

Unit 3

What's* + noun + *like* and answers using *It's . . .

Question			Answer		
What's	the weather	**like?**	**It's**	windy. cold and rainy.	*what's = what is* *it's = it is*

Ask *What's . . . like?* when you want to know the quality or characteristics of something/someone.

1 Read. Circle the word.

1. What day **it's / is** it?
   It's / Is Monday.
2. What's the weather **like / do you like**?
   They're / It's windy.
3. **What / It's** day is it?
   It's / They're Thursday.
4. **How / What's** the weather like?
   They're / It's rainy and cloudy.

2 Look and write.

1. 
   ____________ the weather like?
   ______________________________.
2. 
   What's the weather ____________?
   ______________________________.
3. 
   What ____________ the weather like?
   ______________________________.
4. 
   ____________ weather like?
   ______________________________.

3 **Read.** Write sentences.

S	M	T	W	T	F	S
	Lee's birthday		Mickey's birthday		Janie's birthday	Leah's birthday

1. It's Lee's birthday. ____________? It's Monday.
2. It's Mickey's birthday. ____________? It's Wednesday.
3. It's Janie's birthday. What day is it? ____________.
4. It's Leah's birthday. What day is it? ____________.

4 **Look and write.**

1. 
What's the weather like?
It's rainy.

2. 
____________?
____________.

3. 
____________?
____________.

4. 
____________?
____________.

5 **Write.** Write 3 sentences about today.

____

____

Imperatives

It's rainy.		**Take off**	your	jacket.	*it's = it is*
		Put on	your	boots.	
It's sunny.	**Don't**	**forget**	your	sunglasses.	*don't = do not*

Use the imperative to tell another person what to do.

1 **Read and match.** Draw a line.

1. It's rainy.
2. It's hot.
3. It's cold.
4. It's cloudy.

a. Put on your gloves.
b. Take off your jacket.
c. Take off your sunglasses.
d. Don't forget your umbrella.

2 **Read.** Write a word from the box.

forget	off	on

1. Take ________________ your sneakers.
2. Don't ________________ your boots.
3. Take ________________ your jacket.
4. Put ________________ your gloves.
5. It's rainy today! Don't ________________ your umbrella.

3 Read and write.

1. It's hot. Take off your boots.
2. It's hot. Don't ______ your bathing suit.
3. It's cold. ______ on your coat.
4. It's rainy. ______ forget your umbrella.

4 Look and write.

1.  Don't forget your raincoat.
2. 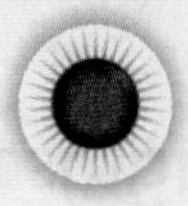 ______.
3.  ______.
4. 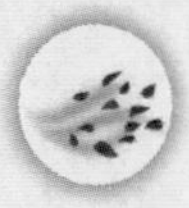 ______.

5 Draw and write. Finish the picture. Then write 3 sentences.

______.

______.

______.

Unit 4

***Like* + infinitive**

	Do	you	**like**	**to play**	soccer?	Yes, I do./No, I don't.
	Does	she				Yes, she does./No, she doesn't.
What	do	you	**like**	**to do**?		I like to play soccer.
	does	she				She likes to play soccer.

1 **Look and write.** Complete the questions.

1. 

What do they like to do ?

3. 

What do you ________________?

2. 

What do they like __________?

4. 

What do they ________________?

2 **Look and write.** Answer the questions in Activity 1.

1. They like to play basketball.
2. They ______________________________.
3. I ______________________________.
4. They ______________________________.

3 Look and write.

1. 

What do they like to do?

They like to play catch.

2. 

______________________________?

______________________________.

3. 

______________________________?

______________________________.

4. 

______________________________?

______________________________.

4 Look and write. Ask questions. Write answers that are true for you.

1. 

Do you like to fly a kite?

Yes, I do. It's fun.

2. 

______________________________?

______________________________.

3. 

______________________________?

______________________________.

4. 

______________________________?

______________________________.

Let's

Let's	watch	a game.	Sure. That sounds fun. ☺
	play	tag.	No, thanks. 😐

1 Read and circle. Match.

1. Let's bounce a ball.
2. Let's catch a ball.
3. Let's play tag.
4. Let's throw a ball.

a. No, **sure / thanks**. I don't like to catch.
b. **Yes, I do. / Sure**. I like to throw a ball.
c. That sounds like **fun / boring**.
d. Sure. I **like / like to** play tag.

2 Look and write.

1. 

Let's bounce a ball.

Sure. I like to play basketball.

2. 

______________________________.

OK. That sounds like fun!

3. 

______________________________.

No, thanks. It's boring.

4. 

______________________________.

OK, sure!

3 **Read and write.** What do you think?

1. Let's throw a ball. ____________________.

2. Let's play soccer. ____________________.

3. Let's color. ____________________.

4. Let's play baseball. ____________________.

4 **Look and write.**

1. Let's talk.
Sure. That sounds like fun!

2. ____________________
____

3. ____________________
____

5 **Write.** It's Saturday. Write 3 sentences about what to do.

Let's play a game. ____________ ____________.

____________. ____________.

Unit 5

Prepositions of place

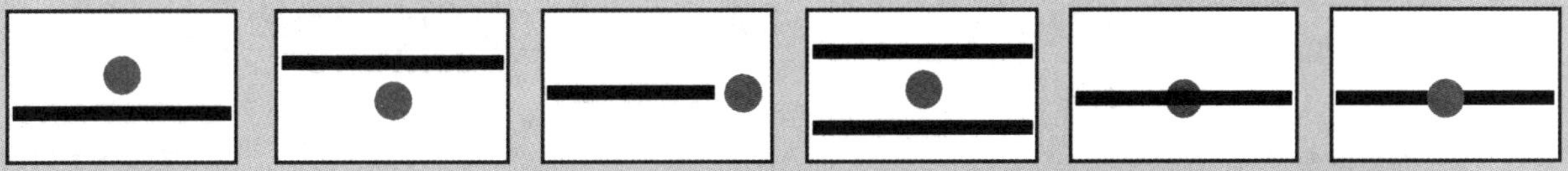

above **under** **next to** **between** **behind** **in front of**

Prepositions of place show how two things are related:

<u>The window</u> is above <u>the table</u>.

1 Look and write.

1.  between
2.  ____________
3.  ____________
4.  ____________
5.  ____________
6.  ____________

2 Read and draw.

1. The picture is above the sofa.
2. The rug is under the chair in the kitchen.
3. The shower is next to the sink in the bathroom.
4. The stairs are behind the chair in the kitchen.
5. The table is in front of the bed.

3 **Look and write.** Complete the sentences.

1. 

The tub is ___under the shelves___.

The shelves are ___above the tub___.

2. 

__________________ the chair.

The chair is __________________.

3. 

__________________ the bookcase.

The bookcase is __________________.

4. 

__________________ the stove.

The stove is __________________.

4 **Draw and write.** Draw a room in your house. Write about it.

____.

____.

____.

____.

Subject-pronoun agreement: *it, they*

Question				Answer				
Where's		the	**bookcase**?	**It**'s	behind	the	sofa.	*where's = where is*
					in	the	living room.	*it's = it is*
Where	are	the	**boots**?	**They**'re	under	the	bed.	*they're = they are*

Use *where* to ask about location.

1 **Write.** Unscramble the dialogues.

1. window / is / where / the ____________________?

   the / is / the / window / above / table ____________________

   ____________________.

2. where / chairs / the / are ____________________?

   room / living / in / the / they're ____________________

   ____________________.

2 **Look and write.**

1. 

   Where's the stove ____________________?

   It's between the door and the sink.

2. 

   ____________________?

   They're in front of the window.

3. 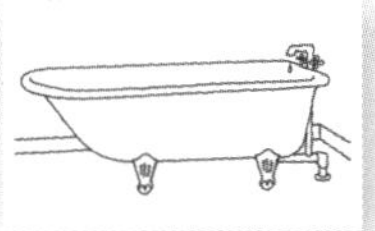

   ____________________?

   It's next to the sink.

4. 

   ____________________?

   They're on the bookcase.

5. 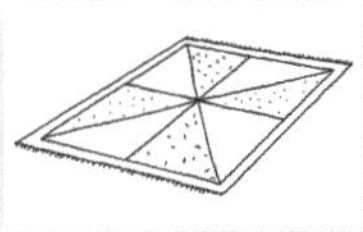

   ____________________?

   It's under the table.

3 **Look and write.** Write questions and answers. Use the words.

1. above Where is the window ?
It's above the sofa .

2. under ______________________?
______________________.

3. between ______________________?
______________________.

4. behind ______________________?
______________________.

5. in front of ______________________?
______________________.

4 **Write.** Write questions and answers about 3 things in your classroom.

Where's the table? It's under the clock.

____

____

____

Unit 6

Telling time

Question					Answer	
What	**time**	is	it?		**It's** 11:00 (eleven o'clock).	*it's = it is*
When		do	you	get up?	**At** 7:00 (seven o'clock).	
		does	she		**At** 8:00 (eight o'clock).	

We often drop *o'clock* when we answer questions about time:
When do you go to bed? At ten.

1 **Read.** Circle the word.

1. **What** / **When** does he eat breakfast?
2. What time **is it** / **it's**?
3. **Is it** / **It's** 5:00.
4. When **does** / **do** she play?
5. **When** / **What** do you eat dinner?
6. **It** / **At** 6:00.

2 **Look and write.** Complete the questions about Manuel's day.

1. 

_________________ eat breakfast?
_______________________________.

2. 
_________________ eat dinner?
_______________________________.

3. 

_________________ eat lunch?
_______________________________.

4. 
_________________ play with friends?
_______________________________.

3 **Look and write.** Ask questions.

1.  When do you get dressed ____________________?

2.  ____________________?

3.  ____________________?

4.  ____________________?

4 **Write.** Give true answers for Activity 3.

1. ____________________.
2. ____________________.
3. ____________________.
4. ____________________.

5 **Write.** Ask and answer about a friend's day.

1. ____________________? ____________.
2. ____________________? ____________.
3. ____________________? ____________.

Adverbs of frequency

Question					Answer
What	do	you	do	**every day**?	I **always** brush my teeth.
	does	your sister	do	in the evening?	She studies. She **never** watches TV.

Always and *never* come after the subject and before the verb in the sentence:
I always go to school. She never plays video games.

1 **Read and match.** Draw a line.

1. What does your sister do on
2. What do you do
3. What does your brother
4. What does your father do in
5. I always

a. every day?
b. the afternoon?
c. Sunday?
d. get dressed before breakfast.
e. do in the evening?

2 **Read.** Circle the words.

1. What do you do **every** / **in** day?
2. What does your grandfather **never** / **every day** do?
3. What do you do **every day** / **always**?
4. I **always play** / **play always** with my friends.

3 **Write.** Answer the questions about people you know.

1. What does your friend always do in the afternoon?

____.

2. What does your teacher never do?

____.

3. What does your mother never do on Saturday?

____.

4 **Look and write.** When does Sandra do each activity? Write questions and answers.

	Monday	Tuesday	Wednesday	Thursday	Friday
1. get up at 6:00	✓	✓	✓	✓	✓
2. ride a bike	✗	✓	✗	✗	✗
3. play with trains	✗	✗	✗	✗	✗
4. go to school	✓	✓	✓	✓	✓

1. What does Sandra do every day ?
   She gets up at 6:00 every day .

2. ______________________________?
   ______________________________.

3. ______________________________?
   ______________________________.

4. ______________________________?
   ______________________________.

5 **Write.** What do you do every day? What do you never do?

____

____

____

Unit 7

***How are you?* with answers *I'm* + adjective**

Question			Answer		
How	**are**	**you?**	I'**m** We'**re**	**OK.** **fine.** **great.**	*I'm = I am* *We're = We are*

He/she looks

You **look** He **looks**	**angry**.	No. I'm bored.
	tired.	Yes. He's busy.
	happy.	Yes. He's always smiling.

Answer the question *How are you?* with *I'm* + adjective (*OK*, *fine*, *great*, *so-so*).

1 **Write.** Unscramble the sentences.

1. are / you / how ______________________________?
2. look / you / surprised ______________________________.
3. they / scared / look ______________________________.
4. looks / bored / she ______________________________.

2 **Read.** Complete the sentences.

1. You __look__ hungry. Yes. __I'm__ hungry.
2. Your mother __________ angry. Yes. __________ angry.
3. Your father __________ bored. Yes. __________ bored.
4. They __________ thirsty. No. __________ hungry.
5. My brother and sister __________ scared. No. __________ surprised.

3 Look and write.

1. 

How are you ?

I'm great !

2. 

?

.

3. 

?

.

4 Look and write.

1.  they/scared

They look scared.

No. They're worried.

2.  you/angry

3.  he/hungry

4.  she/hot

5 **Draw and write.** Draw a face. Write sentences about how the person feels.

Regular and irregular plurals

Plural forms	Singular and plural	More examples
It's my birthday party! Let's cut the cake! The **knives** are next to the **shelves**.	 knife → kni**ves** shelf → shel**ves**	 tooth → t**ee**th foot → f**ee**t sheep → **sheep**
There are some **people** at the party. There are three **men**, three **women**, and five **children**.	person → **people** man → m**e**n woman → wom**e**n child → child**ren**	
My **friends** like to play in the park. They like to fly **kites**.	friend → friend**s** kite → kite**s**	

The regular plural is often formed by adding *s/es* to words, but some plural forms are irregular.

1 Write.

1. shelf shelves
2. toys toy
3. tooth ______
4. foot ______
5. people ______
6. sheep ______

2 **Organize.** Write all of the words from Activity 1.

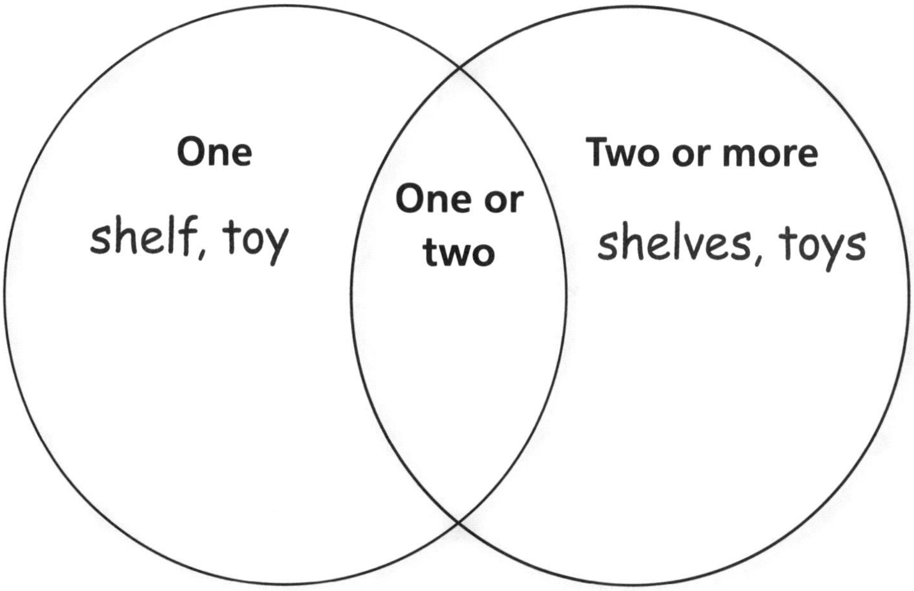

3 **Read and write.** Rewrite the sentences.

1. The girl is crying. The girls are crying.
2. The person looks angry. ______________.
3. The child is yawning. ______________.
4. The sheep is sleeping. ______________.
5. My foot is under the chair. ______________.
6. The baby has one tooth. ______________.

4 **Write.** Use the words. Make sentences.

1. people The people look happy.
2. children ______________.
3. teeth ______________.
4. shelves ______________.

5 **Look and write.** Write 3 sentences about the picture.

____

____

Unit 8

Can and *can't* for ability

A	penguin	**can**	swim.	It	**can't**	fly.	*can't = can not*
Penguins				They			

Question				Answer		
Can	a	penguin	swim?	Yes,	it	**can.**
				No,		**can't.**
Can	penguins		swim?	Yes,	they	**can.**
				No,		**can't.**

Can takes the same form for all persons: *I/you/she/they can run.*

1 **Read.** Write *can* or *can't*.

1. A hippo ________ swim.
2. Zebras ________ run.
3. A lion ________ fly.
4. A parrot ________ swim.
5. Penguins ________ fly.
6. A kangaroo ________ hop.

2 **Write.** Look at Activity 1. Write about each animal.

1. A hippo can swim, but it can't climb.
2. ________________________________.
3. ________________________________.
4. ________________________________.
5. ________________________________.
6. ________________________________.

3 Read and write.

1. Can you play baseball?
   Yes, I can ______.
2. Can your friends play soccer?
   ______.
3. Can your grandfather jump rope?
   ______.
4. Can your mother ride a bike?
   ______.
5. Can a baby run?
   ______.
6. Can you and your friends draw?
   ______.

4 **Look and write.** Write questions for the answers.

1. 
   Can a lion swing? ______
   No, it can't.
2. 
   ______?
   Yes, it can.
3. 
   ______?
   No, it can't.
4. 
   ______?
   Yes, it can.

5 **Write.** What can you do? Write 3 sentences with *can* or *can't*.

______

______

Simple present: *Yes/No* questions with *have* and short answers

Question							Answer			
Does	a	panda	**have**	a	short	tail?	Yes,	it	**does.**	*doesn't = does not*
					long	neck?	No,		**doesn't.**	
Do	pandas		**have**		short	tails?	Yes,	they	**do.**	*don't = do not*
					long	necks?	No,		**don't.**	

The subjects and verbs in a sentence must always be in agreement:

A giraffe <u>has</u> a long neck. Giraffes <u>have</u> long necks.

1 **Read and match.** Draw a line.

1. Do parrots have colorful feathers?
2. Do monkeys have short tails?
3. Does a giraffe have a long trunk?
4. Does a tiger have sharp teeth?

a. Yes, it does.
b. No, they don't.
c. Yes, they do.
d. No, it doesn't.

2 **Read.** Write *do*, *does*, *doesn't*, or *don't*.

1. ____________ a zebra have colorful feathers?

   No, it ____________.

2. ____________ giraffes have long necks?

   Yes, they ____________.

3. ____________ a hippo have big teeth?

   Yes, it ____________.

4. ____________ frogs have long tails?

   No, they ____________.

3 Look and write.

1. 

_________________ colorful feathers?

_________________, they _________________.

Can they fly? _________________.

2. 

_________________ sharp claws?

_________________, it _________________.

Can it climb trees? _________________.

3. 

_________________ a long tail?

_________________, it _________________.

Can it jump? _________________.

4. 

_________________ big teeth?

_________________, they _________________.

Can they fly? _________________.

4 **Write.** Use the words to write a question. Then answer it.

1. elephants / long trunks

   Do elephants have long trunks? Yes, they do.

2. a tiger / feathers

   ____

3. a monkey / a long tail

   ____

4. lions / big teeth

   ____